D1143374

520 998 55 X

COCKER
SPANIEL

INTERPET
PUBLISHING

Introduction

The Cocker Spaniel is now the most popular member of the gundog group of dogs. As well as having a strong instinct to retrieve, Cockers are both highly intelligent and affectionate. The breed was first recognized by the British Kennel Club in 1873. Easy to train and anxious to please, modern Cockers enjoy plenty of exercise and close human companionship. These medium-sized dogs are equally at home in the town or country. They are great with children, adults and the elderly and make wonderful all-round family pets.

Although a Cocker's coat needs quite of bit of grooming, and the breed can be affected by several inheritable diseases, most Cockers enjoy good health and can live for fourteen or fifteen years.

Published by Interpet Publishing,
Vincent Lane, Dorking,
Surrey, RH4 3YX, UK.

© 2014 Interpet Publishing. All rights reserved

ISBN 978 1 84286 249 0

No part of this book may be reproduced or transmitted in any form or by any means, electronic or mechanical, including photocopying, recording, or by any information storage and retrieval system, without permission in writing from the publisher.

Printed and bound in China

The information and recommendations in this book are given without any guarantees on behalf of the author and publisher, who disclaim any liability with the use of this material.

Contents

1 INTRODUCING THE COCKER SPANIEL

The Cocker Spaniel is now the second most popular dog in Britain. It is fifty per cent more popular than the Springer Spaniel, which is the country's third most popular breed. Indeed, for twenty years between the 1930s and 1950s, the Cocker Spaniel was the nation's most popular dog. This is no surprise as the gentle and loving Cocker makes a wonderful companion dog for people of all ages. He is also beautiful and does not need a great deal of exercise. Cockers are also very flexible and are happy to live in either the city or the country. They are very child-friendly and can live up to fourteen years of age. The Merry Cocker is playful, cheerful, amiable, sweet, sensitive and loving. Their soft personalities should always be trained with kind and gentle methods.

For hundreds of years, the Cocker Spaniel's history was inter-mingled with that of all Spaniels. "Spaniel" was a category of dog before being used to describe specific breeds. In early times, spaniels were all born into the same litters and the puppies were then classified according to their size.

LEFT: *A Cocker Spaniel makes a wonderful companion dog.*

Smaller dogs that weighed up to 11.4 kilograms (25 pounds) were designated as Cockers, while larger dogs in the litter would be classified as Springer, Field, Sussex or Clumber Spaniels.

Spaniels were first mentioned in 914 A.D. in the Legal Code written by King Hywel Dda of Wales. He maintained that there were three "higher species of dogs: a tracker; a greyhound; and a spaniel." The King's code deemed that a stolen spaniel was worth three oxen. A few hundred years later, the English poet Godfrey Chaucer compared his famously affectionate character The Wife of Bath to one of these dogs "she coveteth every man she may see, for as a spaynel she wol on him lepe."

Chaucer's French contemporary Gaston de Foix-Bearn, the famous hunting writer, maintained in his book the *Livre de Chasse* that the breed came from Spain, "Spaynels cometh from Spaine... a good Spaniel should not be too rough, but his tail should be rough... they go before their master, running and wagging their tail and raise or start fowl." This is a reference to spaniels being used to flush out and retrieve birds. Another famous hunter,

7

ABOVE: *Cockers can be parti-coloured, in this case, black and white.*

the Prioress of Sopwell Nunnery wrote The Book of St. Albans in 1486. The book was about hawking and hunting and mentions the "spaniel" as being used for both hunting and "comfort." It is said that John Dudley the Duke of Northumberland (1502-1553) was the first hunting marksman to train spaniels to hunt with him. Ultimately, this is how the Cocker Spaniel got its name, as they were used to hunt woodcocks.

In the first ever dog breed book, *De Canis Britannics*, written by Dr. Johannes Caios in 1570, Caios maintained that spaniel originally came from Spain. At this time, most spaniels were white with reddish markings. Red and black dogs were also known but were less common.

In Tudor times, toy and field varieties of spaniel gradually began to diverge. Smaller spaniels were cuddled and petted, and treated as "pretty playfellows" while larger dogs were used for hunting. As time went on the introduction of hunting rifles meant that the role of hunting Spaniels changed from just flushing out game from rough undergrowth to retrieving birds as well.

The first recognized Cocker was the black and tan dog Burdett's Frank. The dog was bred by Francis Burdett. Burdett's Frank was born in 1855. A few years later in 1874 Mr. W. Boulton of Accrington, Lancashire bred an important litter of puppies that included the litter brothers Regent and Regal. Many of today's Cocker Spaniels can trace their antecedents back to these three dogs.

Another famous early Cocker Spaniel, Obo was born in 1879. Nearly all of today's black dogs can trace their roots back to this dog. At the time, black Cocker Spaniels were the most popular. Parti-coloured Cockers are related to the Blue Roan dog Braeside Bustle.

The American Spaniel Club was established in 1881. It was the first American canine club devoted to a single dog breed. Amazingly, Spaniels had first arrived in America on *The Mayflower* in 1620. The ship brought two dogs to the new world, a mastiff and a spaniel. The first American Cocker Spaniel was registered in the late nineteenth century. It was a liver and white dog called Captain. The English Cocker Spaniel Club of America was founded in 1936. By the 1940s the American Cocker Spaniel was smaller, and a separate breed to the English Cocker Spaniel. The American Kennel Club recognized the Cocker Spaniel breed in September 1946.

The British Spaniel Club was founded in 1885 and soon set out the working standard for the breed. The Sporting Spaniel Society was also established. The different kinds of spaniel now began to be more formally categorised. Cocker Spaniels were restricted to weighing less than 11.4 kilograms (25 pounds) and the breed was recognized by the British Kennel Club in 1893. By this time, they were often used to flush out and retrieve game. The Cocker Spaniel Club of Scotland was established in 1933.

These dogs were longer in the body and shorter in the leg than today's Cockers. The first modern-style Cocker was Champion Rivington Ruth, who was born in 1903. Other famous early Cockers included Fairhome Rally (1912), and early Champions of the breed were Ben Bowdler, Bob Bowdler, Invader of Ware and Whoopee of Ware

The biography of perhaps the most famous-ever Cocker Spaniel, *Flush* was published in 1933. Written by Virginia Woolf, the book tells the life story of Elizabeth Barrett

ABOVE: *'Sundust Seeing is Believing' is a show-groomed American Cocker Spaniel.*

ABOVE: *A liver roan Cocker Spaniel.*

ABOVE: *A golden Cocker Spaniel.*

Browning's Cocker Spaniel of the same name. "We cannot doubt that Flush was a pure-bred cocker of the red variety marked by all the characteristic excellences of his kind."

The modern Cocker is a small but sturdy spaniel with a waggy tail that comes in a wide range of seventeen attractive colours and blends of colour. These include the solid colours black, red, golden, black and tan, liver and liver and tan. Cockers can also be parti-coloured. These dogs are either black and white, white and tan, tri-coloured, blue roan, blue roan and tan, liver roan, liver and white, white and tan, orange roan, orange and white or lemon roan in colour.

Cocker Spaniels are now split into two distinct strains, Show and Working Cockers. Show Cocker spaniels are bred to conform to the Kennel Club Breed Standard. This type of Cocker has a domed head, long ears and feathered coat. Show dogs are usually more relaxed than Working Cockers. Working Cockers are the smallest of the sporting spaniels and can make very capable gun dogs. Working Cockers have shorter ears, a flatter skull and their coat has less feathering. Working dogs have more stamina than Show dogs and are very intelligent. This means that they will need more exercise and mental stimulation than their Show dog counterparts.

Working Cockers can make excellent and compact gun dogs, and

ABOVE: *At one time black was the most popular colour for the Cocker Spaniel.*

can be trained to cover the ground within shooting range. Once they have flushed the game, the dog should stop or drop to a sitting position. He should then retrieve on command. Cockers can also retrieve from water. A Working Cocker should have a good ground-covering gait, and be able to move strongly and effortlessly.

Cockers of both strains are lively and intelligent dogs that love to play with their families and their toys. They can excel at obedience and field work.

Tail Docking in Working Cockers

Traditionally, the tails of working Cocker Spaniels were shortened to prevent them from being damaged during their work in thick undergrowth. Such damage might affect the health and welfare of the dog. Surprisingly, Spaniels have actually been depicted with docked tails since the sixteenth century. According to the Kennel Club breed standard for Cocker Spaniels, when the tail is docked, three fifths of the tail should be removed.

Almost all dog tail docking has been illegal in Great Britain since 2007. A few exemptions are made for working dogs, but the criteria are strict and tail docking outside of these exceptions is a criminal offence. The exceptions are defined by the Docking of Working Dogs Tails (England/Wales/Scotland) Regulations of 2007 and the Animal Welfare Act of 2006. It is forbidden to show a dog with a docked tail unless it was born before the ban was introduced. Exemptions to the docking law mean that both docked and undocked Cocker puppies may be available for purchase. Docked puppies have tails that have been shortened within a few days of birth. These docked dogs are left with around two-fifths of the natural tail.

The British Kennel Club breed standard states that an undocked tail should be "set on a line with topline

ABOVE *Cockers are the smallest of the gun dogs.*

LEFT: *Docked Cockers have tails that have been shortened within a few days of birth.*

of back… of a moderate length. Feathering (should be) in proportion to the coat of the dog." A Cocker Spaniel should also have a "merry tail action."

Tail docking has also been banned in Scandinavia and most European countries.

In the United States, tail docking is permissible and is usual for Cocker Spaniel show dogs. Natural tails are considered inconsistent with the official breed standard. According to the American breed standard, "The

docked tail is set on and carried on a line with the topline of the back or slightly higher. When the dog is in motion the tail action is merry."

TEMPERAMENT

Although Cockers have few downsides, they can have one or two habits that can be problematic. The breed is quite prone to submissive urination and Cockers can also be barkers if they are not trained to be quiet. They may also chase birds and should be

ABOVE: *Cockers love families and usually fit in well with other pets.*

taken outside on a leash, especially near roads.

Over breeding has caused the Cocker Spaniel to be subject to various physical and mental health problems. Some dogs are being born with personality difficulties and can be aggressive, shy. Some Cockers may also roam. These dogs need to be especially well socialised. The breed is also prey to several hereditary health problems, some of which can be serious. Please see the chapter about Cocker Spaniel health issues.

For many Cocker Spaniel enthusiasts, the joy of the breed is that the same animal can be both a working hunting or show dog and a great pet. Cheerful, affectionate and highly intelligent, Cockers love their families and like to stick close to their owners. They are great with children and usually fit in well with other pets. Cockers also make excellent house pets, but they do require frequent brushing, combing and clipping of their silky coats to keep them neat and beautiful. They are also prone to shedding. Because of this, Cockers benefit from professional grooming every few months. Having their coats professionally clipped or thinned out will make for easier maintenance. Due to the inquisitive nature of these little dogs and their love of water and mud, regular shampooing may also be

ABOVE: *Cockers require frequent brushing, combing and clipping of their silky coats to keep them neat and beautiful.*

necessary. The hair between their paw pads and on top of the feet should be kept short to keep the feet clean around the house. This also means that there will be less chance of thorns and burrs getting stuck in the hair and making the dog uncomfortable.

Cockers' intelligence and sociable personalities mean that they need to be kept well socialised and occupied to keep them happy and well-behaved. Dogs that are left alone for long periods of time, or unoccupied, may resort to mischievous and destructive behaviour or they may become nuisance barkers. Separation anxiety is a condition that affects many dogs from this breed, and it is definitely unkind to leave Cockers alone for long periods of time.

Although most Cockers are very good natured, a minority can become aggressive and/or dominant as they mature. There have been rare incidences of the so-called "Rage" syndrome in Cockers. This problem has also been reported in American Cocker Spaniels, Bernese Mountain Dogs, Chesapeake Bay Retrievers, Dobermans, English Bull Terriers, English Springer Spaniels, German Shepherds, Golden Retrievers, Pyrenean Mountain Dogs and St. Bernards. Although the number of affected animals is very small, the condition is thought to be genetic in origin and inheritable. It seems to be more prevalent in red and golden-coloured dogs, but this probably just reflects the fact that the condition is carried by certain bloodlines. Multi-coloured dogs seem less susceptible. During an attack of "Rage" a dog will suddenly act aggressively to anyone nearby, but minutes later it will be calm and normal. The dog does not seem to remember what has happened and may be friendly to the person it attacked in the immediate aftermath. Unfortunately, these attacks cannot be prevented with training because the "Rage" is not under the dog's conscious control. Attacks happen without apparent cause, although an individual dog may have a specific trigger, such as being woken up unexpectedly. Prior to an attack the dog's eyes may glaze over and the dog may then become snappy before it attacks. "Rage" can only be thoroughly diagnosed by a vet using an EEG or genetic testing and even these tests can be inconclusive. A variety of treatments including anti-epileptic drugs have been reported to be effective, but not every treatment works for every dog. Although "Rage" is a serious problem if it manifests itself, it is worth remembering that only a very small number of Cocker Spaniels are affected.

RIGHT: *Most Cocker Spanish are very good natured.*

2 CHOOSING YOUR COCKER SPANIEL

Cocker Spaniel puppies are so adorable that it is extremely tempting to scoop up one (or two!) and take them home. But getting any dog is a serious undertaking and you should be sure that you really want a dog (any dog) and that a Cocker Spaniel is the right dog for you. The issue of having time to exercise and give your dog the companionship he deserves is particularly critical to Cocker ownership.

Most people buy Cocker Spaniels as family pets, but parents should be aware that they will almost inevitably end up looking after the dog, and will certainly be financially responsible. You should also remember that a Cocker Spaniel can live for fourteen or fifteen years, and you will need to commit to him for the whole of that time.

Once you have decided that you would like to take a Cocker Spaniel into your life, the next big decision is whether a Working or Show dog would be right for you. The gene pools of Field and Show Cockers have now been separate for about seventy years, and both types have different strengths to offer their new family.

Most Cockers have characteristics of both aspects of their heritage. They have the toughness and ingenuity of hunting dogs but are also kind and cuddly household pets.

LEFT: *A Cocker has a lifespan of fourteen or fifteen years.*

Working Cocker Spaniels

ABOVE: *A working Cocker will enjoy an active life.*

If you are hoping to get a dog that will come shooting with you, a Working Cocker would certainly be preferable. Although Working Cocker Spaniels are highly intelligent and easy to train, they have a lot of energy and need to be kept busy to be happy. However, if you lead an active life a Working Cocker might be ideal. Like all Spaniels, the Cocker is a people-orientated dog and doesn't tend to latch on to a single individual, but if you train him to be a gundog, he will feel closer to his hunting companion. Working Cocker Spaniels have also become popular competitors at canine sports such as Canine Agility and Flyball.

Physically, Working Cockers tend to have flatter skulls and higher set, shorter ears than show Cockers who have a more domed skull and longer, lower set ears. Another big difference is in the coat. Although some working type dogs have heavy coats they usually have finer hair and less feathering than Show Cockers.

Show Cocker Spaniels

If you want to show your dog, or if you want an easy-going family pet, a Show Cocker Spaniel might be the best option. They are usually slightly more compact than working dogs, but need more grooming with their thicker, longer coats. Daily grooming and washing may well be necessary. You should be able to pass a comb easily through his coat. If you want to show your dog, you will definitely need to buy from a reputable Show line.

ABOVE: *Show Cockers are more compact than working dogs.*

Dog or Bitch?

ABOVE: *Male and female Cockers both make excellent pets.*

The personality differences between male and female Cockers are quite subtle, and both sexes make excellent pets and hunting partners. Bitches are usually slightly quieter, and may be easier to train and quicker to housetrain than dogs. On the other hand, if you get a dog you won't have to cope with their seasons every six to eleven months (solid coloured Cockers seem to have more frequent seasons), unless you have your bitch spayed. During her season (eight to sixteen days) you will need to keep your bitch away from male dogs. To make doubly sure that there are no unwanted pregnancies, you should do this for approximately three weeks. A bitch in season will also have a bloody discharge that may stain your furniture. Cocker bitches come into their first season at widely varying ages, from as young as nine months up to thirty months of age.

If your male Cocker is unneutered, you should make sure that your garden

21

is secure in case he scents an on-heat bitch in the neighbourhood! It is surprising how normally mild-mannered dogs will suddenly jump over fences or even out of windows when their hormones take over.

Male Cockers are usually slightly larger and heavier than bitches, and can be more exuberant. But they almost always have great characters and are reasonably trainable, as well as being loving and faithful. Although many Cocker owners maintain that bitches are more easily trainable, they can be a little more demanding, with their own agendas. In mixed-sex households, it is usually Cocker bitches who are the leaders of the pack. Bitches have a stronger pack drive and desire to be part of the group. They tend to make better leaders with their managing skills.

Both male and female Cockers sometimes engage in scent marking (with small amounts of urine). This is more common with male dogs and is usually associated with dogs trying to assert their dominance in the canine/human pack. This problem can be resolved with good training and by the dog's owner/s assuming the dominant role in the family.

If you are buying a Cocker to be your hunting companion, a dog may be preferable as otherwise you will need to leave your in-season bitch at home for the duration of her bi-annual season.

In short, both Cocker dogs and bitches can make wonderful pets, and (with the correct training) they can live harmoniously together.

BELOW: *If your male Cocker is unneutered, you should make sure that your garden is secure in case he scents an on-heat bitch.*

Puppy or Older Dog?

One of the great things about adopting a grown-up Cocker Spaniel is that you are probably giving a home to a dog that really needs one. There are many rescue organisations with dogs available for adoption in Britain, the United States and Canada. There will also be advantages to you. Your older dog may well be house trained and may also have been taught how to walk on the lead, and ride in the car. An older Cocker Spaniel may also be more appropriate for an elderly or infirm owner. You will also be able to see exactly what you are getting in the way of temperament and size.

The best way to find an older Cocker Spaniel may be through a breed rescue organisation. Dogs can end up in rescue kennels for many reasons, most of which are no fault of the dog. For example, the dog's owner may have died or become ill, or a dog bought for showing may not have reached the required standard. Breeding bitches and stud dogs may also have been retired and would hugely benefit from having a loving and relaxed home of their own. One of the great things about Cocker Spaniels is that because they are such people-loving dogs, they will soon adapt to you and your lifestyle. An older dog might also find it easier if you are not at home all day and probably won't be as needy as a puppy.

ABOVE: *An older dog will probably have learnt how to walk on a lead and ride in a car.*

23

Finding a Breeder

If you decide to buy a puppy Cocker Spaniel, you will need to find a highly regarded breeder. One of the best ways to do this is to contact a Cocker Spaniel breed club. Breed clubs often have lists of litters that have been bred by their members. If you can, it is highly desirable to meet the breeder before you decide to buy. A good breeder will want to know that you can offer a good home to one of their puppies and you can see the conditions in which your pup has been bred. They will also want to be reassured that a Cocker Spaniel is the right dog for you. A responsible breeder should ask many questions about your home environment and lifestyle. If they do not feel that you can offer one of their puppies a good home, they may even refuse to sell you one.

A good breeder will also be knowledgeable about the hereditary conditions that can affect the breed. They should have made sure that their breeding stock has had annual eye tests, has been hip-scored, and has been DNA tested for PRCD-PRA and FN kidney disease. A responsible breeder may well have only one or two litters each year, so you may need to be patient and plan for your puppy.

Another good way of contacting breeders is to visit dog shows where Cocker Spaniels are being shown. This would also give a wonderful opportunity of meeting some Cockers close up and seeing the different sexes, sizes, and colours of the breed. The UK Kennel Club also has an Assured Breeder scheme where their members can offer litters on-line through their website. This is an excellent way of buying a dog for showing if that is your ambition. Most good breeders will also be a member of at least one breed club such as The Cocker Spaniel Club and will probably be active in promoting this lovely breed.

But the very best way to find your puppy is by personal recommendation from someone who has already bought a puppy from a breeder. Naturally, if you are looking for a Cocker Spaniel to be a loving pet and companion, you need to look for a puppy from an affectionate and healthy environment.

Alternatively, if you want your puppy to grow into a show dog, you should try to source your puppy from a successful kennel. Breeders who sell budding show puppies will be well-placed to advise you about the potential of their puppies and give you an idea of how they will develop. A show puppy should appear balanced

ABOVE: *You may be able to visit your puppy once or twice before he is ready to go home with you at about eight weeks of age.*

and attractive, and carry himself well. But buying a show puppy is always tricky. A puppy that looks like he has loads of potential at eight weeks of age may have faded by the time he attends his first dog show at six months.

If you are lucky enough to find a litter that has the kind of pup you are looking for, it can be a great bonding experience to meet your future puppy a couple of times before you take him home with you. It will also give you a chance to meet the parents of your puppy (or the dam at least) and this will give you an idea of how your dog will develop. You can also keep an eye on him to make sure that he stays in good health before you pick him up. This should be at around eight weeks old. A good breeder will be happy to welcome you to see your puppy and will be pleased by your interest.

Choosing Your Puppy

Once you have found a litter from which to choose your puppy, you need to use some objectivity to choose the right dog for you. In fact, there's no point in looking at a litter prior to five weeks of age. You need to see the puppies on their feet before you can judge them properly. If possible, it would be great to see the puppies' mother and father. The main points to look for are your puppy's physical and behavioural health. So far as his physical health goes, there are several things that you should look out for. The puppy should have a good level of energy, and appear alert and interested in his surroundings. His eyes should be bright and clear without any crust or discharge, and he should be able to see a ball that rolls by slowly. He should look well fed, and have a little fat over his ribs. A healthy puppy's bottom should be free from faeces. His coat should be flat and glossy and not scurfy, dull or greasy. There should be no evidence of fleas or lice in his coat. He should be able to walk freely without any limping or discomfort. The puppy should be able to hear you if you clap behind his head.

So far as his behaviour goes, you should look for a puppy that seems to be interacting well with his littermates - playing nicely without being too assertive. The puppy should also be interested in playing with you and should approach you willingly. He should be happy about being handled, and let you cuddle him and touch him all over his body. If he remains calm and relaxed while you do this, he is likely to be easier to handle when he grows up. You should remember that each puppy has a unique personality and there are perfectly valid reasons why a puppy may look less friendly and engaging at a first glance. For example, he may just have woken up or be feeling sleepy. At eight weeks of age a Cocker Spaniel should be calm and reasonably assertive. He shouldn't appear to be too spooked by noises, and should calm down quickly if there is a sudden noise.

It's worth remembering that around sixty per cent of your Cocker's personality will have been inherited, while forty per cent will be acquired as a result of his socialisation and training. Although it is to be hoped that the breeder will have given the puppies the best possible start in life, surrounded by care and love, you will have the biggest part to play in your puppy's future development and a great opportunity to shape his personality.

PUPPY LAYETTE

Before you collect your puppy Cocker Spaniel, you will need to equip yourself with some simple pup-friendly equipment. His requirements will include a bed, basket, or dog crate a puppy collar and lead, a grooming brush, safe, durable puppy-friendly toys and puppy food (as per the breeder's instructions). It is well worth investing in a special spaniel water bowl. These heavy earthenware pots are tapered towards the top to stop your Cocker's ears falling into the water. Stainless steel dishes are ideal for their food and won't be chewed.

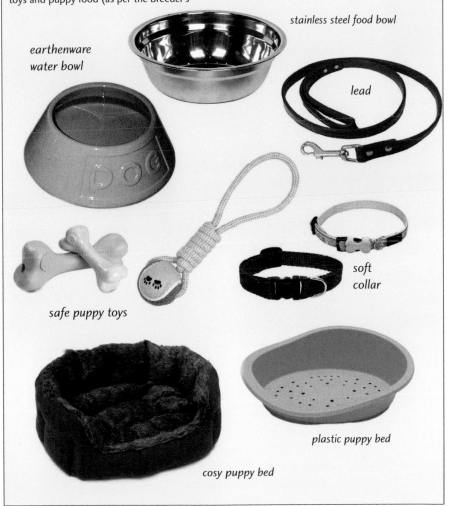

stainless steel food bowl

earthenware water bowl

lead

safe puppy toys

soft collar

cosy puppy bed

plastic puppy bed

Preparing for Your Puppy

You will need to make some important preparations before you collect your Cocker puppy and bring him home. You need to decide where you want your puppy to sleep, eat and exercise and which parts of your house you will allow the puppy to go. Consistent behaviour on your part will help your puppy feel secure and settle down quickly, so start as you mean to go on. All dogs need to have a routine and it is best to get this established as soon as possible.

Before you collect your puppy

DANGEROUS PLANTS FOR DOGS

Many house and garden plants are also highly toxic to dogs and puppies, and you should be very careful to keep them away from your Cocker Spaniel. Of course puppies are much more likely to chew unsuitable things, so you need to be particularly careful that they are not exposed to a whole list of dangerous plant materials including:

ABOVE: *Bluebells are beautiful to look at but dangerous if your dog eats them.*

Aconites	Bluebells	Cocoa husks *(used in garden mulches)*	Onions
African Violets	Box wood		Ragwort
Apple seeds	Buttercups	Daffodil bulbs	Rhubarb
Apricot stones	Cherry stones	Elephant ears	Wild cherry
Crocuses	Christmas roses	Ivy	Yew
Avocado	Clematis	Mistletoe	

you must make sure that his new environment is free of any hidden hazards. Very importantly, your garden needs to be well fenced. A little Cocker puppy needs only a tiny hole to squeeze through. Any openwork gates should have wire mesh attached, and any dangerous garden equipment should be put away. Ponds are a particular hazard for puppies. If they fall in, they may well be unable to climb out. Indoors, you must make sure that electrical cables and phone wires are concealed.

It is a good idea to put away anything that you don't want to be chewed. You won't want to be telling off your new puppy on his first day in his new home. It might be a good idea to confine your small Cocker to a metal or plastic puppy pen to keep him as safe as possible.

One of the most important things to decide is where your puppy is going to sleep. This is crucial as this is somewhere that your puppy needs to feel completely safe and secure. It should be a place that suits you and the dog. The most important thing is that the sleeping area should be warm, dry and completely draught free. Many owners prefer their new puppies to sleep in the kitchen or utility room as these rooms usually have washable floors. But you should not let him sleep in a confined space where there is a boiler in case of carbon monoxide leaks. You could also fence off a small

area around the basket with his puppy pen so that your puppy won't be able to get into trouble in the night. A dog crate or cage can also make your dog feel comfortable and secure. If you leave the door open, your dog can also use the crate as his refuge during the day. Dog crates are also useful to keep your dog confined and safe during car journeys. You should never use the crate to punish your dog, as he should always want to go into it and feel comfortable there.

Although there are many different kinds of dog beds on the market, the simple plastic kidney-shaped baskets, which come in many different sizes and colours, are among the most practical. They resist chewing and can be washed and disinfected. They can also be filled with cosy pads or mattresses on which the puppy can sleep comfortably. These mattress inserts can usually be washed in the washing machine. It's a good idea to buy two in case of accidents! An excellent idea is to replace the fabric softener in the washing cycle with a slug of disinfectant to make sure that any germs or bad smells are destroyed. Wicker baskets can be dangerous when chewed as the sharp sticks can damage the puppy's mouth or throat. Equally, bean bag beds can easily be chewed through and the polystyrene beans they contain are difficult to clean up. Dog duvets are equally prone to chewing.

Collecting Your Puppy

ABOVE: *Your puppy will have to adjust to his new home and sleeping alone for the first time.*

The best age to collect your puppy is when he is around eight weeks old. When you arrange a time to pick him up from the breeder, a time around mid-morning is often the most convenient. This will give the puppy a good chance to feel at home by bedtime. He will be able to sniff around his new home, be cuddled by his new owners, eat, play and sleep before he faces the night alone.

It's a good idea to take someone with you when you go to collect your Cocker Spaniel puppy, so that one of you can drive and the other one can comfort the pup. An old towel to mop up any accidents is a good idea. When you collect him, make sure that you find out when he will need his next worming treatment and what vaccinations he has already had. You should also receive a copy of your puppy Cocker's pedigree. You should also take this opportunity to check that he is still in good health, with clear eyes, normal motions, shiny hair and normal weight.

Although it is a very exciting time when you bring your Cocker Spaniel puppy home for the first time, you should try to keep the atmosphere as calm and reassuring as possible. Moving to his new home is a complete change for your puppy and he has to fit into a completely new environment. If there are other animals in your home you should always supervise the puppy until they have settled down together. Alternatively, if you are bringing an older dog into your home, he may already have insecurities that you will need to dispel.

LIFE CHANGES

Your puppy will have a lot of things to adjust to. At first, he may well feel lonely without his littermates around him. A hot water bottle wrapped up in a blanket and a cuddly toy may help. Beware of going to your puppy if he cries during his first night with you. This is giving him the message that you will come running whenever he cries. You may also be tempted to take a miserable puppy into your own bed which you may not want to do in the long-term. A half-way house is to allow the puppy to sleep in a high-sided box in your bedroom so that you can comfort any crying. The box will mean that he has to stay put and can't get into difficulties or fall down the stairs. After a couple of days, you can move the puppy into the kitchen.

If you are re-homing an older dog, be sure to call him by the name he is used to. Trying to change it to something you prefer will confuse and upset him.

BELOW: *If you home an older dog, don't confuse him by renaming him.*

3 CARING FOR YOUR COCKER

VACCINATIONS

One of the first and most important things you need to do for your Cocker Spaniel puppy is to make sure that he is enrolled into a comprehensive vaccination programme. This will protect him against the serious illnesses of distemper, hepatitis, parvovirus, leptospirosis, and kennel cough. He will need regular boosters throughout his life. You should keep your puppy at home until he is fully protected.

Puppies should be vaccinated at 6–9 weeks of age and then again at 10–12 weeks. Puppies will usually become fully protected two weeks after the second vaccination but your vet may recommend a third dose for some puppies. The vaccine your vet will use will contain a modified dose of the disease that will stimulate your dog's immune system to produce antibodies that will be able to fight the disease. If your puppy is unwell, it may be a good idea to postpone his injections for a while, to minimise the small risk of an adverse reaction. Most vaccines are injected into the scruff, but the kennel cough vaccine is given as drops into the nose. This is usually only given to dogs that will be left in boarding kennels, but it may also be useful if your dog needs to go into hospital for any reason.

When you take your unvaccinated puppy to the vet, you should make sure that you carry him and do not put him down in the surgery. If you plan to put your dog into a boarding kennel, you will need to keep an up-to-date card showing the vaccinations he has had.

RIGHT: *Carry your puppy to the vet for his first vaccination as he will only be fully protected two weeks after the second shot.*

ABOVE: *Your Cocker will need regular booster vaccinations throughout his life.*

ABOVE: *Make sure you supervise your puppy as he explores his new home.*

PUPPY NUTRITION

Another of the other most important things you can do for your puppy Cocker is to feed him well. If you have bought your dog from a responsible breeder, they should have given you a diet sheet to follow. If you don't know what your puppy has been eating, you need to buy him some suitable puppy food. These foods are now sometimes breed-specific. It is important that your puppy has access to water at all times but even more so if you are feeding dry food, as these foods can make your dog very thirsty. A common mistake is to give cows' milk to a puppy. This can badly upset his stomach and give him diarrhoea. Goat's milk is much more palatable to dogs, as it is lower

in lactose (to which many dogs are intolerant) and higher in protein. This means that it is much closer to bitch's milk. Fully-weaned puppies don't need milk of any kind.

As your puppy only has a small tummy, you will need to divide your puppy's food into several small meals. Four meals are usually considered best for puppies up to the age of twelve weeks old; breakfast, lunch, tea, and supper. Serving small meals at 7a.m., 11a.m., 3p.m., and 6 or 7p.m. works quite well. Don't allow your puppy Cocker to go without food for long hours in the day. Leave his food down for around ten minutes so that he learns to eat up reasonably quickly. Don't worry if he doesn't finish his food at this age, he may just be full. Dried food will swell in the puppy's tummy and he will soon feel satisfied. Leaving his food down for him to graze on is not very salubrious. At this age, intervals of three to four hours between his meals should be about right. Once your puppy is three months old, he can move to three meals a day. By the time he is six months old, two daily meals will be sufficient. When your dog reaches his first birthday, you can move to a single daily meal if you like, but many people prefer to divide their dog's food into two meals a day. If you are unhappy feeding your dog a complete dry diet, you can always supplement this with some tasty treats.

Most Cockers have great appetites, and crave tidbits. You shouldn't struggle to get your puppy eating heartily. But other puppies seem quite uninterested in food and you may worry that he's not getting enough. It may well help if you hand feed your puppy for a while, as Cockers will often take food from your hand that they would ignore in their bowls. They undoubtedly love the extra attention this brings. Although modern complete diets are extremely convenient, and contain everything your puppy needs, some owners prefer a more traditional puppy diet of various nutritious foods. You should not rely on a diet of household scraps as it is very unlikely that this will provide enough nutrition for your puppy to grow up strong

ABOVE: *Dry puppy food should be measured out according to the guide on the packet.*

and healthy. If you decide to feed a traditional meat and biscuit diet rather than a complete food, you should be sure to give your dog a vitamin and mineral supplement each day.

Many Cockers put on a little excess weight as they age. As this puts extra strain on their hearts, this should be prevented if at all possible. Swapping some of his food for cooked green vegetables or changing to a lower calorie version of his usual food should help. You should never give your dog human goodies as these can also damage his teeth. Stick to dog treats and dog biscuits.

ABOVE: *Frozen carrot chunks make a healthy dog treat.*

ABOVE: *Most experts recommend that Cockers should not be taken on long walks until they are around a year old.*

PUPPY EXERCISE

Your new Cocker puppy needs to be kept both mentally and physically active to make sure he is stimulated and happy. But he should not be taken out in public until at least two weeks after his final vaccination. Playing in the garden will be fine at this stage. But it is very important to exercise your Cocker puppy in moderation as his bones are still soft and growing. Over-exercising a puppy can lead to damage and he will also tire quickly. Most experts recommend that Cockers should not be taken on long walks until they are around a year old.

As your Cocker matures, exercise will become an increasingly important part of his day. Although he will appreciate long walks, he will also appreciate variety and having a free run. You can also take toys with you on his walk, so that you can play with these as you go.

PUPPY TOYS

Because Cockers like to chew it is important to make sure that anything you give your puppy has been tested for its resilience. Pull toys might spoil his teeth, so these may be best avoided. Squeaky toys should have the squeaker removed in case this gets swallowed. Small balls are also dangerous. Large balls and chew toys made out of tough rubber are best and homemade toys such as cardboard boxes will give your puppy hours of harmless fun.

WORMING

All dogs have worms at some point in their lives, and puppies are at the most risk from infestation. Worms are passed from the mother even before birth and through their milk. They then live in the puppy's intestine and feed on partly digested food. Untreated worms can cause serious illnesses in puppies, including weight loss, vomiting, diarrhoea, a swollen tummy and even death. An infested puppy cannot get the benefit from his food and will not thrive. He may also cough

ABOVE: *Large balls made out of tough rubber are safe toys for your Cocker.*

and his coat may look dull. Puppies need regular worming to combat this and should be wormed from two weeks of age at two weekly intervals until they are twelve weeks of age, then every month until they are six months of age. Worming should continue at least three times a year with a recommended veterinary preparation for the rest of the dog's life.

Dogs are prone to two main types of worms, tapeworms and roundworms. Roundworms can appear like elastic bands, up to several inches in length.

ABOVE: *Socialise your puppy with other dogs as soon as he is protected by vaccination.*

ABOVE: *Make worming a regular treatment for the whole of your Cocker's life.*

Tapeworms can appear like white grains of rice, which are joined together to form a tape. These are most commonly found in adult dogs and very rarely in puppies.

Your breeder should tell you about the worming programme they have been using and when the next treatment is due. It may be a good plan to let your puppy settle down before you worm him again. Twelve weeks is usually considered to be a good age for this. Your vet can recommend a good product to use. Roundworms are spread through the environment while tapeworms are commonly spread by fleas, so it is wise to treat an infested dog with a flea treatment. Climate change has meant that dogs are now subject to new types of worm, Angiostrongylus, for example. These worms can live in the lungs or in the major blood vessels and may even cause death. Ordinary worming medicine does not work against these parasites. You should check with your vet to see which worms are problematic locally.

One of the first things to do with your new Cocker puppy is to get him used to being handled, this is very important so that you can do essential things such as clean his teeth and cut his nails.

Personal Care for Your Cocker Spaniel

ABOVE: *Your Cocker's coat will require a lot of grooming but this liver Cocker youngster is loving every minute.*

TEETH CLEANING

A Cocker will usually get his adult teeth at around the age of four-and-a-half months. You need to check which puppy teeth are loose and which have fallen out, and to see how the new ones are coming on. Gently lift the lips to check the teeth. Be especially careful if your puppy is teething. It is good to get your puppy used to this procedure so that both you and your vet will be able to examine his mouth without too much trouble. You should check the tongue to make sure that it looks normal, and check the dog's teeth and gums. The teeth should be clean and free from tartar. If tartar builds up on the teeth his breath will smell, the teeth will become discoloured and eventually the gums will be affected, leading to infection. Unfortunately, Cocker Spaniels are particularly prone to periodontal disease because the teeth are quite close together. As Cockers can live to a good age, it is particularly important to look after their teeth so that they can last for a lifetime.

You can clean your dog's teeth with a special canine toothbrush, or a small piece of gauze wrapped around your finger. You can get special dog toothpaste from your vet (or on-line). This comes in various tasty flavours, such as chicken. Alternatively, you can use a paste of baking soda and water. Don't use fluoride toothpaste on puppies under the age of six months, as this can interfere with the formation of his dental enamel. Human toothpaste should also be avoided as this can upset your dog's stomach.

Teeth cleaning chews and rawhide toys can help keep the tartar build up down. Your vet may also recommend special hard food to help keep your dog's teeth in good condition.

EYE CARE

Your Cocker's eyes should always be bright and clear and free from any foreign objects. You need to check your dog's eyes regularly as eye problems can be indicative of other health problems. You should watch out for excessive crustiness, tearing, red or white eyelid linings, tear-stained hair, closed eyes, cloudiness, a visible third eyelid, or unequal pupil size. If you see of these eye symptoms, you should contact your vet immediately.

NAIL CLIPPING

Unless your Cocker Spaniel spends a lot of time walking on hard surfaces that will help to keep his claws short, his nails will need regular clipping. If you hear them clicking on a hard surface, it's time for a trim. Most dogs dislike having their feet handled, so you should try to get your puppy used to this from an early age. A dog's claw is made up of the nail itself, and the quick, which provides the blood supply to the nail. Avoid cutting into the quick as it will bleed profusely and is very

ABOVE: *Gently lift the lips to check the teeth.*

41

GROOMING KIT FOR COCKERS

It is worth investing in a small set of good quality grooming equipment. This should include:

- A steel fine-tooth comb
- A slicker brush
- A hard bristle brush
- Nail clippers

- A pair of straight scissors
- Electric clippers
- Tissues
- A piece of chamois leather or silk

steel comb

bristle brush

slicker brush

nail clippers

straight scissors

electric clippers

chamois

sensitive. Don't worry if you can't cut all your dog's nails in one session, it might be best to clip one paw at a time, with other activities in between.

GROOMING

One of the best features about the Cocker Spaniel is the breed's lovely coat. This should be long, silky and glamorous. The downside is that their coats do need quite a lot of work, especially if you intend to show your dog.

An un-clipped Cocker will require daily brushing to keep his coat clean, especially after walks where his long coat can pick up all kinds of dirt and rubbish. He needs a good brushing all over, with special attention to his feathering. You should also give your Cocker a thorough brushing before you bathe him.

The sooner you start to groom your Cocker puppy, the sooner he will get used to this kind of handling. This is vital if you want to show your dog. A Cocker will usually have his adult coat by the time he is ten months old. Most dogs really enjoy the care and attention they receive while they are being groomed. The best way to start is to stand your dog on a firm surface that won't wobble. A table or work top is ideal. Start your grooming session by using the hound glove or a brush to remove all the dead hair and foreign objects from his coat. The comb will come in handy when you are tidying the feathers on his legs and ears. Be as gentle as you can during this process. You should groom inside and outside his ears, being very gentle and careful not to scratch the delicate skin in this area. Once you have finished brushing him, it is a good idea to wipe around his eyes with a damp tissue. Once he has his longer adult coat, you can buff

ABOVE: *Take the opportunity when grooming to check your Cocker for lumps or scratches.*

this to a shine with the chamois or a piece of silk.

A well-groomed dog does not need regular bathing. This tends to strip the natural oils from his coat. But if your Cocker has rolled in something horrid, you probably won't feel you have a choice. A squirt of tomato sauce applied to the dirty area and then washed out will get rid of any dreadful smells. When washing your Cocker, you should use a canine shampoo and make sure that this doesn't wash into his eyes. Use lukewarm water to wash the dog, and make sure that you thoroughly rinse the soap out of his hair. Try to squeeze as much water out of his coat as possible before lifting him out of the bath. Once you have towelled him dry (or dried him with

43

BELOW: *Most dogs really enjoy the care and attention they receive while they are being groomed.*

hairs in your dog's coat. These hairs come away quite easily and removing them will not cause your dog any discomfort. Your cocker should be plucked on the top of the head, the muzzle, shoulders, back, sides, behind the elbows, the front of the front legs, the outside of the rear legs, the feathers, the rump, the tail feathers and the rear pasterns.

The best way to strip the dead hairs is to take several strands of the longer, protruding hairs between your thumb and forefinger. You can then very gently pull out the longest hairs. Fully stripping your dog may take several hours, but you should make sure that he has regular breaks so that he does not get bored or de-hydrated. You should aim to strip his coat around every two to three weeks.

a hand-held hairdryer) you should brush out his coat. It is much easier to do this if you place your dog on a raised surface to do this. If you use a hair dryer, try to brush and dry him simultaneously.

Cockers' hair grows very quickly and your dog will need regular trimming to keep his coat in good order. If you want to show him, this will need to be done very precisely, possibly professionally. But if you are keeping your dog as a pet you may wish to do it yourself.

Traditionally, Cockers are partly stripped and partly clipped. Stripping his coat is usually done by hand. It is much easier to do this before you bathe your dog, but you can use powdered chalk to get a better grip on clean hair. Stripping or plucking is designed to get rid of the dead

The more delicate areas of your dog's body should be very carefully trimmed with thinning scissors. These areas include the throat, around the anus, the underside of the paws, the back of the hock, the ends of the feathers and the hair inside the ears. Learning to trim your Cocker Spaniel may take some time. The result you should be aiming for is for your dog to look as natural as possible.

Although your dog will not care what he looks like, having a well groomed coat will mean that he is much more happy and comfortable and the fact that air can get to his skin will keep it much healthier.

Unwanted Visitors

Unfortunately, a Cocker's luxurious coat seems to be the ideal home for several parasites including fleas, lice, ticks, ear mites and harvest mites.

FLEAS

Fleas are small, flat, wingless, blood-sucking insects that are an irritation to dogs and their owners alike. They can also can carry and transmit serious diseases and other parasites (such as tapeworms). They are also the leading cause of skin problems in domestic dogs. Although they can't fly, fleas have powerful rear legs and can jump to extraordinary lengths. There are many types of flea, all of which reproduce rapidly and profusely. Despite its name, the ordinary cat flea is by far the most common flea that bothers pet dogs. Dogs become infested if good flea prevention isn't followed. Dogs can also get fleas by having contact with other animals that have a flea problem. Fortunately, there are many things that dog owners can do to keep fleas under control. Most dogs that have fleas will find them irritating and will scratch, but some can have a severe reaction to flea bites (flea dermatitis). If you think that

BELOW: *The luxurious coat of a Cocker is a potential home for all sorts of parasite.*

you have found flea debris in your dog's coat, collect some of the black grit from the coat and put it on a white tissue. If the black grit goes blood-coloured when you dampen it, your dog has fleas. Wash the dog as quickly as possible, not forgetting his bedding and around the house. There are many excellent flea-control preparations on the market today, but your vet will probably be able to sell you the most effective.

TICKS

Ticks can sometimes be found in your dog's coat in the summer months. Ticks are parasites of sheep and cattle. The adult tick starts life small and spider-like. It crawls over the body, finds a suitable place and bites into the skin. It will stay in this position for about two weeks until fully engorged with blood, swollen to the size of a pea and beige in colour. The tick will then drop off the host and, if female, lay eggs in the grass. These hatch into larvae which will then find a host. After a feed, these larvae drop off, undergo change and find another host. It takes three larvae changes, each taking a year, before the adult form is arrived at and the cycle is then repeated. Ticks can be removed by using flea-control remedies, some of which are also designed to remove ticks. Other methods involve removing the tick with special forceps, making sure you grasp the head. This is made easier by killing the tick first. If you don't manage to remove the tick's mouth parts, the bite can become infected.

ABOVE: *Walks in the countryside are fun but in summer you should always check your dog's coat for ticks afterwards.*

ABOVE: *Check ears for ear mites.*

LICE

Lice are grey, about 2mm long and they lay small eggs (nits) which stick to the dog's hair and can look like scurf. Dogs can then scratch and create bald patches. You should give your dog repeat treatments of insecticide sprays or baths to kill the adults and any hatching larvae. They can often appear in a Cocker's ears.

HARVEST MITES

Harvest mites infestation occurs in the late summer, starting around late July. They are little orange mites which affect the feet, legs and skin of the tummy and can cause immense irritation. The orange mite can just be seen with a naked eye. Treat with benzyl benzoate, a white emulsion which can be bought at the chemist, which should be rubbed into the affected parts. Many of the flea insecticides will also treat this complaint.

EAR MITES

A Cocker Spaniel's heavy ear flaps can stop a good circulation of air around his ears. Waxy deposits in this area may mean that he had ear mites, especially if he is scratching. Ear drops can get rid of them and regular application should keep them away.

Cocker Spaniel Health Issues

Although uncommon, Cocker Spaniels can be affected by a range of hereditary health problems. These can be serious and veterinary advice will be required. These include:

PATELLA LUXATION

Patella Luxation (or slipping of the kneecap) is usually caused by a genetic deformity of the knee joint. It causes difficulty in straightening the knee, pain in the joint and limping. Normally, less severe cases are treated with painkillers, while surgery may be necessary for more seriously deformed joints.

HIP DYSPLASIA

Hip dysplasia or CHD is a serious condition that affects several breeds of dog, including Cockers. This degenerative condition affects the hip joint of the hind legs and can be crippling. A puppy can be born with seemingly normal hips, but the symptoms of the condition can appear as he matures. The condition can cause pain and lameness. It can be diagnosed by an X-ray.

SPINAL PROBLEMS

Unfortunately, Cocker Spaniels are genetically prone to Intervertebral disk disease. This can result in slipped discs, degenerated discs or herniated discs. Male dogs are more likely to have disc degeneration than bitches. Factors that increase the risk of disc degeneration include genetic predisposition, excessive weight and lack of muscular fitness.

FN KIDNEY DISEASE

Famial Nephropathy (FN) kidney disease is a recessively inherited renal disease that has been known to affect Cocker Spaniels for more than fifty years. The kidneys of affected dogs can begin to deteriorate at a very young age. This devastating illness can be diagnosed by protein being passed in the dog's urine. Nearly all FN affected dogs will have symptoms of the illness by the age of one. Renal failure usually happens between the age of six months and two years. A DNA test was introduced in 2006 that identifies carriers of the condition and affected dogs should never be bred from.

INHERITED GLAUCOMA

Glaucoma is a serious condition that can affect several breeds of dog including Cocker Spaniels. Blindness can result. Affected eyes can look as protuberant. The condition can result in a medical emergency, but if diagnosed it can be controlled by drugs. Where this doesn't fully control the condition, surgery may be required to prevent pain and blindness. A gonioscopy test for a pre-disposition to this condition is available, and dogs with condition should not be bred from.

Cockers are also prone to several other diseases of the eyes: inward-growing eyelashes, inward rolling eyelids, outward rolling eyelids, third eyelid problems, retinal problems and cataracts. If these problems are not diagnosed at an early stage, there may be permanent damage to the eyes. Any signs of squinting, eye redness, ocular discharges, pawing at the eye or cloudiness warrant a veterinary examination.

PROGRESSIVE RETINAL ATROPHY

FPRA (Progressive Retinal Atrophy), also known as GPRA. A DNA test is available for this condition.

Progressive Retinal Atrophy (PRA) is an inherited eye disease found in many breeds of dogs, including Cocker Spaniels. The condition has varying ages of onset. There are various types of PRA but the one most commonly seen in Cockers is GPRA (General Progressive Retinal Atrophy or prcd-PRA). The condition results in night blindness, which may lead to total blindness. In Cockers, PRA has a variable age of onset, from as early as eighteen months to as late as seven years. It is inherited via a recessive gene, meaning that a copy of the defective gene must be inherited from both parents for the disease to occur.

ENTROPION

Entropion is a painful condition in which a dog's eyelids roll inward, allowing the eyelashes to rub against the cornea and irritate it. The upper and/or lower eyelids can be involved, and the condition can occur in either one eye or both. A dog with entropion will squint and have an excessive amount of tears coming from the affected eye. While any dog can have entropion, there is often a genetic factor. When caused by genetics, the condition will show up before a dog's first birthday.

ABOVE: *Cocker owners have to be vigilant for signs of eye disease in their pet.*

INHERITED CATARCTS

Cataracts are caused when a dog's eye lens hardens and becomes opaque, interfering with the dog's vision. The only treatment for canine cataracts is surgery.

SKIN PROBLEM

Cocker Spaniels are prone to various skin conditions. These include primary seborrhea. This over-production of skin oils results in greasy and scaly skin that can have a bad smell. The condition can be diagnosed by biopsy and treated with vitamin A derivatives and anti-fungals to control any secondary yeast infection. Regular use of anti-seborrhoeic shampoos and moisturizers can also control the condition.

Cocker Spaniels can also suffer from food allergies. These can often cause itchiness and red and swollen skin in the dog's ears and feet. Food allergies can also cause gastrointestinal symptoms. They can be diagnosed by an elimination diet, but it may take some time to find the offending foodstuff, up to eight to twelve weeks. Once the problem food is identified it can be avoided in the dog's diet.

AUTOIMMUNE HEMOLYTIC ANAEMIA

Cocker Spaniels have a predisposition for autoimmune hemolytic anaemia or AIHA. The condition causes the dog's own immune system to attack its blood cells. Symptoms include pale gums, fatigue, and jaundice. The dog may also develop an enlarged liver that can result in a swollen stomach. Diagnosis is made by physical examination and blood tests. Treatments include the use of steroids to suppress the immune response. The dog may also need a blood transfer or chemotherapy. Sometimes it can be fatal. Cockers with AIHA should not be bred from.

HYPOTHYROIDISM

Cocker Spaniels are also prone to hypothyroidism and autoimmune hypothyroidism. The conditions cause the antibodies of the dog's immune system to attack their thyroid hormones and the thyroid gland itself. The result is that the dog's body fails to produce enough thyroid hormone. Symptoms can include thyroid tumours, a slow metabolism, hypothermia, dry skin and excessive shedding or hair loss. Darkening of the skin and itching may also occur. Serious cases may result in infertility and a thickening of the skin that gives the dog's face a puffy appearance. A severely affected dog may even lapse into a coma. Hypothyroidism can be diagnosed by a blood test and treated with replacement thyroid hormone.

DEAFNESS

Both English and American Cocker Spaniels have been reported with cases of congenital deafness. It seems to be more common in white dogs with blue eyes. This form of deafness is caused shortly after birth by the degeneration of blood supply to the inner ear or cochlea. It is permanent and may affect one or both ears. A puppy that fails to wake up during a loud noise is likely to have bilateral deafness. The brain stem auditory evoked response (BAER) test is used to diagnose deafness in dogs. Bilaterally deaf dogs are difficult to train and may develop behavioural problems as they are easily startled. Deaf Cocker Spaniels should not be bred from.

Common Canine Ailments

Anal glands: A dog's anal glands are located on either side of the anus. Their original use was for scent marking. As a rule these glands are emptied by defecation but, if the dog's motions are soft and too loose, there is not the pressure on the glands which is needed to clear them. An affected dog will drag his rear end along the floor, or will attempt to chew or lick near his tail area in order to relieve the irritation caused by overfilled anal glands. An abscess may occur if they are not cleaned. If you are unable to empty them yourself, it would be advisable to get your vet to do it for the dog's comfort.

Arthritis: This is a complaint that usually affects older dogs. A veteran Cocker may endure stiffness, but do not allow the dog to suffer

ABOVE: *If you are worried about your puppy's healthy check with the vet as soon as possible.*

unnecessarily as there are several remedies that greatly benefit this complaint.

Burns and scalds: The treatment for burns and scalds is the same as for humans. Rinse the affected area under a cold tap or hosepipe in order to take the heat out; if necessary, cut away as much hair as possible. In minor cases apply a suitable soothing ointment; in serious cases your vet must be consulted. A badly burned dog will be suffering from shock and should be kept warm and quiet in his bed or box.

Constipation: If this happens frequently it probably indicates incorrect feeding, so you may want to adjust your feeding regime. Gnawing bones can also cause this problem in some dogs. Changing your dog's exercise patterns can sometimes cause constipation. Dogs are creatures of habit and, if they have to wait too long to pass a motion, this can cause constipation. When a dog is constipated, occasionally it will pass a smearing of blood with the motion. As long as it is only a trace it will resolve itself but, if there is any considerable amount then it should be considered serious. Home remedies for an odd incident of constipation include a small amount of olive oil, mineral oil, or milk. You should also make sure that your dog is drinking enough as this in itself can cause constipation. If the attack lasts for longer than twenty four hours or the dog seems to be straining excessively, you should consult your vet immediately as this may indicate a blockage.

Diarrhoea: There can be many reasons for this condition. The dog's diet, a change of diet, or eating something nasty can start a bout of diarrhoea. This can usually be stopped by fasting the dog for twenty-four hours. You should give him a solution of glucose and water to drink so that he does not become dehydrated. Start feeding again with light, easy-to-digest foods such as chicken or fish. Diarrhoea can also be a sign of serious problems such as gastroenteritis, parvovirus, worm infestation, foreign bodies in the gut or internal organ problems. Stress can also trigger diarrhoea, just as it does in humans. You should monitor your dog closely while he suffers from diarrhoea, and if a bout turns into something more persistent you should take him to the vet. Unattended diarrhoea can lead to your dog becoming dehydrated and extremely ill.

Fits: There are a considerable number of reasons why dogs fit. Puppies that are infested with worms can fit. Once de-wormed they never fit again. Puppies may also have a reaction to their vaccinations and this can bring on a fit. This is rare but you should report it to your vet. He should be able to correct the problem. A fitting dog can be a very distressing sight. He may collapse, and may froth at the mouth. He may also go rigid and his legs may start to move as though he is running. He may also lose control over his bladder and bowels. While this is happening do not interfere, but ensure the dog can do no harm to himself while thrashing about. When the dog comes out of a fit he will be extremely weak and confused and will stand and walk as if drunk. Put the dog, at this point, in a safe, enclosed, darkened place where he will be quiet until he has recovered. If the dog has another fit you should definitely take him to your vet. If epilepsy is diagnosed there are drugs that will control it.

Heatstroke: This is an acute emergency which happens during hot weather. It mostly occurs in dogs that have been shut inside a hot car. A dog should never be put in a hot car in warm weather, even with the windows well open. A car will turn into an oven on a warm day and the temperature inside the car will increase rapidly. A dog can become severely distressed in minutes and die very, very quickly. Even on much cooler days the windows must be left wide open and grills fitted. A heatstroke victim will be severely distressed, frantically panting and will probably collapse. His temperature will be extremely high and, to bring it down, the dog's body should be submerged in cool water or hosed down with water. Do not use very cold water as this will cause more problems. When the temperature returns to normal the dog should be dried and put in a cool place to recover. The dog should have drinking water available at all stages, preferably with salt added (one dessertspoonful of salt per litre of water). If the dog does not recover quickly it would be advisable to take him to the vet as he may be suffering from shock.

Lameness: Dogs will go lame for many reasons but the most common causes are found in the foot. If your dog is lame, check the pads for cuts, cracks, dried mud between the pads, thistles or any kind of swelling. Check the nails have not been damaged or that the nail bed is not infected. Sores between the pads can also cause lameness. If you find a foreign body in the foot, remove it and clean the foot with warm antiseptic water. An infected nail bed will need antibiotic treatment from the vet. This condition is very painful and should be treated quickly. If it isn't treated, the nail can drop off, which can cause further serious problems. A damaged nail, if down to the nail bed, should be bandaged to stop the dog knocking it further. Be extremely careful when you bandage your dog's feet. This can do serious harm if it is done incorrectly. Get professional help if in doubt.

If nothing appears wrong in the foot you must start to go up the leg, feeling for any swellings, lumps or cuts. Feel the opposite leg and compare the shape and size. Find out if there is any difference in the heat of the legs; bend the joints and move the leg. The dog may or may not flinch when you touch the injury. Some dogs will be lame one day and, after resting overnight, will be completely sound the next. However, if the cause of your dog's lameness is still undetected and has not improved after two days you should take him to your vet.

The Veteran Cocker Spaniel

A Cocker Spaniel has an average life expectancy of between twelve and fifteen years. Birth to two years old is usually considered to be the growth stage, two years to five years old the young adult stage, five to eight years middle age, and eight years plus old age. Of course, as any dog gets older he may well need more day-to-day care and veterinary treatment.

To many owners their veteran Cocker Spaniel becomes even more precious as he ages. He will have given the best years of his life to be your companion. There are still some lovely times that you can have together as Cockers can live to a good age.

As your dog ages his needs will change and the way you care for him will need to keep up with this. Good sense will tell you how much exercise he wants. A dog over the age of eight should be taken for shorter walks at his own pace. Of course, each dog will age at his own rate, so discretion and discernment is required.

Diet is perhaps one of the important changes you will notice as your dog ages. He will no longer require as much food. Teeth may not be as good as they were, so an entirely hard diet may no longer be suitable. It might also suit your older dog to eat two smaller meals each day so that his digestive system can cope better. Many dog food manufacturers offer diets that have been specially designed for the older dog. These may well be appropriate for your older Cocker.

If your dog is taking less exercise you may also find that you need to trim his nails more often, and you need to make absolutely sure that you keep his coat clean and comfortable. Grooming will also give you a chance to check him over and notice any health problems at an early stage.

Older Cockers should always be kept comfortable and warm. You should never allow your older dog to get cold and wet. Make sure his bed is somewhere where the temperature is constant and free of draughts. He will sleep longer and more soundly than when he was younger. If you have younger dogs in the family make sure the old dog is not left out but, at the same time, do not let the young dogs either annoy or disturb the old dog when he is sleeping. You should also protect the old dog from any over-boisterous activities from the younger dogs.

Although every day with your dog is precious, if your Cocker is failing in health and losing his quality of life you may need to consider putting him to sleep. Your vet will help you make that decision when the time comes. It is the hardest decision to make but don't let your dog suffer at the end; you owe it to him to have a dignified and painless departure from the world.

BELOW: *Protect your older dog from the boisterous attentions of younger dogs.*

4 TRAINING YOUR COCKER SPANIEL

Basic obedience is important for any dog, but Cocker Spaniels are sweet and biddable and will want to please you. The first few weeks after you bring your puppy home are important in setting the tone of your future relationship. It will be completely unnecessary to smack your dog, or punish him in any way. A sharp tone of voice and a firm "No!" should be sufficient. He is young and although he will certainly make mistakes, he will never be naughty on purpose. If he makes mistakes, you need to forgive and correct him gently. As your puppy grows, it may be a good idea to enroll him in local obedience classes, but you can start his training the moment you bring him home to live with you.

HOUSE TRAINING

House training is the first sort of training that you should begin with your puppy. It should begin as soon as you first arrive home with him. With vigilance and positive training methods, most puppies quickly learn how to be clean in the house. Being a highly intelligent breed, Cockers are particularly quick to learn.

House training will be easier if your puppy has a settled routine, sleeping and eating at the same times during the day. Puppies usually need to relieve themselves when they wake up, during play, and after meals. You should also watch for signs indicating that your puppy wants to go to the toilet; restlessness, whining, tail raising, sniffing and circling around. You should take your puppy to the same place in the garden on each of these occasions. You should encourage him with a consistent phrase such as "toilet." As soon as the puppy performs you should praise him and play with him. You may be surprised how often your puppy needs to relieve himself, but remember he has only a small bladder at this age. This means that he will find it very difficult to stay clean all night long, so it may be a good idea to leave some newspaper or purpose made absorbent pads (available from your local pet shop) down at night.

If your puppy makes a mistake you need to clean up as well as you can so that no smell lingers. Any lingering odour might give the puppy the idea that he can use that spot for his "business" in the future. While some puppies are easier to house train than others, you should remember that your puppy will not have full bladder control

ABOVE: *After short periods of training you can reward your Cocker with a game.*

until he is about four months old and should never be punished for making mistakes.

NAME TRAINING

The very first thing is to teach your puppy his name. You need to call him over to you with a treat in your hand, or be ready to play. You should sound excited and praise him lavishly when he comes to you. A small tidbit works well for Cockers! If you try to establish "coming when called" at an early age this will become second nature to him, and may save his life in a dangerous situation. It's a good idea to have imprinted this lesson on your dog before allowing him any free range exercise.

TEACHING RECALL

If you are struggling to get your puppy to come to you, try carrying a treat in a crinkly paper bag. If your puppy doesn't come when you call him you can rustle the bag while you repeat his name. As soon as he has made the connection between the rustling paper and the treat he will always come to you. When he does you should stroke and praise him.

If your Cocker decides to disobey you use a low firm voice to get his attention. You don't need to shout! Once you have it you should immediately change your tone to a soft and encouraging tone and call him again. This should do the trick. When he has obeyed you give him a treat and praise him. You should also remember that however angry your dog has made you by refusing to come when he has been called, you must never punish him when he does finally come to you. This will confuse him and undermine his trust in your leadership.

A recall lead is useful for this exercise once you are ready to practise in an open space.

TRAINING TIPS

Before you move on to the next steps of training your puppy to sit, stay and walk to heel etc. there are some basic training tips that it are well worth remembering.

You should always make sure that you have your puppy's attention before you give a command. You should aim only to give commands that your puppy will obey, so you need to make sure that he is listening to you. You can do this by calling his name or snapping your fingers until you have good eye contact with him. Then give your command and make sure that your puppy follows through. Give him time to respond but ensure that he does as you have asked. Don't keep repeating the command as this means that your pup chooses when he obeys you. The idea is that he should obey you at once.

Puppies have only a short attention span, so you should keep your training sessions to no more than five or ten minutes. Your puppy won't be able to focus for much longer than this. It's important to keep the atmosphere of the training sessions as positive as possible, with lots of praise. If your puppy seems confused by a new command go back to something you know he can do so that you can end the session on a positive note. If you are using training treats as part of your method you may well find that it's better to time your sessions before meals, when the puppy might be a little hungry. But as your puppy gradually learns your commands you should phase out the treats, as you don't want to have to rely on treats in the long term.

In training your dog you should try to step into the role of being a positive pack leader or good parent to your dog. Bonding with your dog in his early life and encouraging him to mix with other people and animals will help him to be calm and confident when he grows up. Because he will not be protected by his vaccinations in these early weeks you will need to carry him if he goes outside your house and garden. Your attitude is very crucial at this stage in his life. If he has your calm and unqualified support, it will help him to develop into the kind of well socialised dog who will be easy to train.

LEAD TRAINING

Most Cockers learn how to walk on the lead quite quickly. Their natural inclination is to keep close to you so attaching a lead to your pup's collar is usually no problem. Twelve to fourteen weeks is a good age for a puppy to start wearing his first collar. The puppy's neck will be very soft and delicate so you should use a very soft and comfortable collar. Your puppy will soon grow out of this, so wait until he is at least six months of age before you buy him anything expensive.

The best place to begin training your puppy is in your garden. In this safe and controlled environment your puppy can learn about walking on the lead where there is nothing to upset or distract him. Encourage him and praise him as he walks well, but do not allow him to rush forwards and pull. If he does, keep calm and talk to him, then persuade him to walk a few steps and praise again. It will not take long for him to learn. Calm lead work will build a strong bond of trust between you so that when he goes out into the world and meets new and scary things he will look to you for reassurance. You have several weeks to work on this exercise before his vaccinations are complete and he can go into the outside world.

TRAINING TO HEEL

The art of training your Cocker to "heel" is a simple extension of training your puppy to work on the lead. The greater control the exercise gives you over your puppy is particularly important in an urban environment. A head collar or anti-pull harness can be helpful during heelwork training. The

ABOVE: *Start the heel exercise with your dog close to your left leg.*

object of the exercise is to have the puppy walking by your side with his head level with your left leg.

Start the exercise with your dog close to your left leg, with both of you facing the same way. Have one of your pup's favourite treats in your left hand. Hold the treat up near your waist, not directly in front of your dog's nose. Now say your dog's name to get his attention and to gain eye contact. Immediately take two steps forward and then stop. If your dog moves with you and is still in the heel position enthusiastically praise him and give a treat.

As soon as your puppy swallows his reward repeat the heeling process again. Say his name and take two steps

Staffordshire Bull Terriers as Therapy Dogs

Staffies love people so much that they can make great Pets As Therapy (PAT) dogs after the appropriate training. Therapy dogs are usually trained from puppies to be "bombproof" by being exposed to lots of different situations, people and noises. Therapy dogs work with all kinds of different people, including the elderly, disabled and sick. Their loving and kind natures are ideal for this kind of important work and contact with these dogs can be very healing and beneficial.

ABOVE: *Learning the commands for down and stay will be useful for you and your dog.*

several times the puppy will go down without you having to put your hand to the floor, but reward and praise every time until it is firmly established. If the puppy will not go down at the start of this training you can give very gentle pressure on the forequarters to encourage him to go down to the floor.

TEACHING THE STAY

Learning to "Stay" is important to all dogs. When you first start to teach your puppy to stay it is best to have him on the lead. Ask the puppy to either sit, or go down, with the lead extended from you to the puppy; walk away backwards (facing the puppy) and repeat the command "Stay". When you get as far as the end of the lead, stand still for a few seconds, ask the puppy to come, and praise him. Gradually lengthen the distance you leave the puppy and always give praise when he does it right. If the puppy breaks the Stay take him back to where you left him at Sit or Down and repeat the exercise, but do not go so far away from him before you call him. This exercise will take time and patience; little and often is best. It may be helpful if you use a hand signal as well as the command.

5 COCKER SPORTS

As well as working in the field, Cocker Spaniels also take part in several different kinds of canine competitions, including mini-agility, Flyball, tracking and obedience.

COMPETITIVE OBEDIENCE

Many Cockers take part in competitive obedience trials at dog shows around the world. This rewarding sport is the logical extension of good training. Each level of obedience trial has a set list of exercises and requirements for dogs and their handlers to follow as closely as possible. Marks are awarded for the ability of the combined dog/handler team. As well as taking your dog's training to a higher level, competitive obedience can be highly enjoyable for both dogs and humans and a great bonding experience.

MINI-AGILITY

Cockers are naturally suited to agility competitions. They want to work with their handlers and obey their instructions. Their small size gives them an advantage over bigger dogs on obstacles such as the tunnels, dog walk and see-saw. You shouldn't allow your Cocker to attempt an agility course until he is fully grown, or at least a year old. Mini-agility is a scaled down version of agility designed for smaller dogs like the Cocker.

Competitive agility and mini-agility date back to the Crufts dog shows of the late 1970s. To entertain the audience in the interval dogs ran around a specially designed course against the clock. The inspiration behind the concept was competitive horse jumping. The sport quickly spread to the United States and has now spread around the world. The sport consists of a dog and handler running around an obstacle course together. The obstacles are usually all different, but may include a variety of hurdles, an A-frame, a dog-walk, a see-saw, a tunnel, a long jump and a tyre. The competing dog/handler teams are scored for speed and accuracy. The dogs participate off the lead and it is not permissible to encourage them with food or toys. The handler can only use voice and hand signals to instruct their dog.

FLYBALL

Cockers can also make great Flyball competitors. They love to play and this is a great opportunity for young and fit dogs to play and socialise. As well as keeping Cockers and their owners fit, competing in Flyball can help to build

63

the rapport between dog and owner.
Flyball is a modern variant of canine agility that has become very popular in recent years. Essentially, Flyball is a sport in which teams of four dogs run in relays over a line of hurdles to a box where the dogs collect a tennis ball that they then return to their handlers. In Britain it is governed by the British Flyball Association and in America the sport is regulated by the North American Flyball Association.

ABOVE: *Flyball is an enjoyable relay team sport for dogs and owners alike.*

Gundog Training

If you want to train your Cocker as a gundog it would be wise to buy a dog from the correct stock. Cocker Spaniels make some of the best gundogs in the world. Your Working Cocker's pedigree should include Field Trial Champions and Field Trial Winners. These titles may be abbreviated as FT Ch. or FTW. These dogs are usually smaller than their Show Dog counterparts. A puppy from a good background will very likely have a natural retrieving ability and a good nose to find game. Chances are that he will also have pace and stamina and be able to cope with both cover and water. Today's gun dogs are trained to find, flush and retrieve game. Cockers were bred to work as gundogs and training your dog for this purpose is a great way of channelling his natural bounce and energy. In the UK the Gundog Club manages a graded training scheme for gundogs that was launched in 2006. Many pet Cockers have now joined this scheme on their way to becoming fully-trained gundogs. The scheme is suitable for pet dogs, working dogs and even Show dogs. All true Cockers have the instinct to retrieve and the training capitalises on their natural instincts. These intelligent dogs enjoy this kind of challenging training and working together will help you form a

great bond of mutual respect with your dog. Many people have no intention of using their dog in the field when they start gundog training, although they may change their minds when they see how this work comes so naturally to their Cocker.

In the first place, the best way to get your dog's training off to a good start is to join your local Gundog club. The good news is that you don't need to be a landowner to train a gundog. Most Gundog clubs will have access to a suitable piece of land, with differing terrain, where your dog can learn his new skills. This will include learning to retrieve, scent discrimination and walking to heel off the lead.

The equipment you will need to get started is minimal – just a gundog slip-lead and a half kilo canvas training dummy. These can be found at country shows, gun shops or on-line.

Learning to Retrieve

The lively and intelligent Cocker has a variety of in-born skills and retrieving is one of them. But what if your puppy just doesn't seem interested in playing fetch? Even though nearly all Cockers are born with an instinct to retrieve, it sometimes takes a little time and training to jumpstart this natural impulse. It might also be the case that, for a teething puppy who is still cutting his adult teeth, picking up objects with his mouth might be uncomfortable. Most Cockers start to become more interested in retrieving at about six months old. Whether you are working with a puppy or an adult Cocker Spaniel the first step is to toss his toys and see if your pup shows an interest in running after them. It's more convenient to play this game in an enclosed area, like a hallway, where the dog can't avoid you after fetching the toy. When your dog brings the toy back to you ask him to sit and gently take the toy from him. Then praise him and give him the toy back.

Once you have graduated from these first attempts to a training class, you and the other trainee handlers will be asked to make a line with your dogs. Dummies will then be thrown for you. Your job is to get your dog to wait until you are asked to retrieve the dummy. As soon as he does so you should make him sit still in front of you and gently take the dummy from him before giving him lots of praise. This training will continue until your dog can also retrieve hidden dummies, double dummies and dummies floating on water. As his tuition becomes more advanced your instructor may also encourage you to use a whistle, your voice and hand signals to communicate with your dog.

If you want to use your Cocker as a gundog your pup will also need to become acclimatised to loud bangs and noises so that he won't be frightened by gunfire. A starter pistol that fires blanks can be a good way to introduce the noise of gunfire into the dog's environment. Try to "fire" at some distance from the dog, getting slowly closer.

As well as retrieving your gundog's training should include learning how to "quarter." This means working systematically in a zigzag pattern, covering the area ahead of you, while he is controlled by hand and whistled signals.

When your dog has matured a little, by about the age of around six months, you can attempt some more advanced training techniques including retrieving hidden dummies, retrieving from water and jump fences.

If you want to use your dog in the field you should be sure that he knows not to chase game or livestock. The final stage of training your dog to work in the field is to begin shooting over your dog. This is probably the most crucial stage of gun dog training. Of course, this is potentially very dangerous, with even fatal consequences, so you really need to have expert tuition or experienced peer mentoring at this stage.

Many people have no intention of using their dogs for live shoots, but aim to train their dogs to a level where they can participate in field trials. Most field trial societies and clubs schedule special categories for puppies and novices as well as for more experienced dogs. Competing for the first time can be quite intimidating, but a good Field Trial society will try to make new members feel welcome.

TRACKING

Cockers retain enough of their sporting heritage to enable them to be very good tracking dogs. In tracking competitions, a dog follows a scent trail laid by someone walking over the ground. The dog must keep closely to the original track. He may get some help from air scent, but to succeed the dog must keep its head close to the ground. As the handler doesn't know where the track has been laid, he must learn to trust his Cocker and be able to read his body language.

Therapy Cocker Spaniels

LEFT: *The gentle and affectionate Cocker makes a wonderful therapy dog.*

BELOW: *Therapy dogs are trained from puppyhood and exposed to lots of different people and situations.*

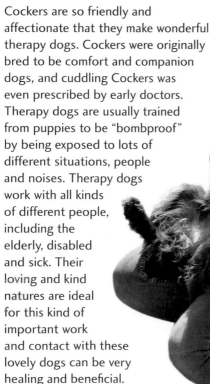

Cockers are so friendly and affectionate that they make wonderful therapy dogs. Cockers were originally bred to be comfort and companion dogs, and cuddling Cockers was even prescribed by early doctors. Therapy dogs are usually trained from puppies to be "bombproof" by being exposed to lots of different situations, people and noises. Therapy dogs work with all kinds of different people, including the elderly, disabled and sick. Their loving and kind natures are ideal for this kind of important work and contact with these lovely dogs can be very healing and beneficial.

68

6 SHOWING YOUR COCKER SPANIEL

If you bought your Cocker puppy from a line of show dogs, you may wish to show him. This will mean that your dog will be compared to the Cocker Spaniel breed standard. This lays down the ideal character, temperament and appearance for the breed by which your dog will be judged.

The first thing that any good judge will be looking for is a sound and healthy dog that is a good example of the breed. No reputable breeder would allow an unhealthy dog, or a dog with health issues to produce a litter.

COCKER SPANIEL BREED STANDARD

A good Cocker should have a merry nature with a waggy tail and a bustling movement, particularly when following a scent. Cockers are fearless of heavy cover.

Temperamentally, Cockers are gentle and affectionate but full of life and exuberance.

Dogs should be approximately 39 to 41 centimeters tall (around 15 to 16 inches). Bitches should be 38 to 39 centimeters tall (or 15 to 15½ inches). A Cocker Spaniel should weigh between 13 and 14.5 kilograms (28 to 32 pounds).

A wide range of different coat colours is acceptable for Cocker Spaniels in the show ring. These include several solid colours: black, red, golden, liver (or chocolate), black and tan and liver and tan. Solid coloured dogs may have slight white markings on the chest. Parti-coloured Cockers include black and white, orange and white, liver and white and lemon and white dogs, which can be with or without ticking. Tri-coloured Cockers can be black, white and tan or liver, white and tan. There are also six different varieties of roan Cocker Spaniel: blue roan, orange roan, lemon roan, liver roan, blue roan and tan and liver roan and tan.

The coat itself should be flat and silky in texture. It should not be wiry, wavy, overly profuse or curly. A Cocker should be well feathered on his forelegs, on the hind legs above the

69

hocks and on the body.

Facially, Cocker's have square muzzles with a distinct stop set midway between the tip of the nose and the occiput (the back of the skull). They have well-developed skulls which are cleanly chiseled but neither too fine nor too coarse. The Cocker's cheek bones are not prominent but the nose is wide enough to get a good scent. His eyes are full and round, but not prominent. Brown or dark brown in colour a cocker's eyes should never be light in colour. Liver, liver roan and liver and white dogs have dark hazel-coloured eyes. The eyes should have an intelligent and gentle expression and should be merry and bright.

The Cocker's ears should be lobular and set low, on a level with the dog's eyes. The ears should have fine feathers that extend to the tip of the nose. They should be well covered with long silky hair. His mouth should be strong-jawed with a complete scissor bite.

ABOVE: *You may find it safe and convenient to take your dog to shows in a dog crate.*

He should have a clean throat and his neck should be muscular and moderate in length and set into his fine sloping shoulders.

The Cocker should have sloping shoulders and well-boned, straight legs that give him power in the field. These shouldn't be too short. His body should be strong and compact with a well-developed chest and deep brisket. He should be neither to narrow or wide across the front and his ribs should be well sprung. His sides should be short and wide with a firm and level top-line that slopes gently to the tail. The tail should be set slightly lower than the back and have the characteristically merry action of a Cocker. His hindquarters should be wide, rounded and very muscular. His back legs should be well boned and have plenty of drive. His paws should be firm and thickly padded.

Cocker Spaniel dogs should also have two normal testicles fully descended into the scrotum.

DOG SHOWS

Showing your dog can be a great way to make new friends and can be a highly absorbing hobby. There are all kinds of dog shows from the informal to the highly competitive and there are also parallel events for young dog handlers. So long as you approach dog shows with good sportsmanship and a sense of humour they can be great fun. You will need a small amount of

ABOVE: *The judge will want to see him in action moving around the show ring.*

equipment to show your dog. This should include a good grooming kit, a show lead, and a water bowl. You may find it safe and convenient to take your dog to shows in a dog crate. At the show itself the judge will want to check your dog over and see him in action moving around the show ring. In Britain all dog shows are regulated by the Kennel Club.

Before you show your own dog it is a very good idea to attend a dog show and see what will be expected of you and your Cocker. This may give you an idea of how the dogs are prepared for showing. Bathing a day or so before the show should keep coat smart and pearly white. He will then need a thorough grooming, especially around the feathers.

ENTERING A SHOW
Most dog shows ask their participants to fill in a set of entry forms. You need to fill in these show entry forms very carefully, as mistakes may mean disqualification. In the UK your dog also needs to be Kennel Club-registered in your name before you can show him. Novice owners may think that if a dog has been registered by the breeder he can be shown. But this is not the case. Make sure that you arrive at the show in good time so that you and your Cocker can settle down in the busy atmosphere and relax.

IN THE RING

All dog show judges have their own system of judging, but most judges will ask participants to line up as a class. The judge will then ask you all to move together before inspecting the dogs individually. They will then ask you to move your dog on his own so that he can give him a full inspection. Most judges start their examination at the dog's head. This will include looking at your Cocker's mouth to see if he has the breed's correct bite. The judge will feel the body, forequarters and hindquarters. He will also check your dog's paws, pads and his tail. The judge, with both hands, will span the dog behind the shoulders and lift him briefly to assess his weight.

The judge will then ask you to move the dog around the ring. He might ask you to move up and down, or in a triangle. This is so that he can assess the dog's movement from the front and rear and in profile. When the judge has reached a decision, he will place the dogs in order of merit. Don't take it too badly if you don't win on this occasion, you and your Cocker Spaniel may be more lucky next time you venture into the show ring.

ABOVE: *A Cocker should be well feathered on his forelegs, on the hind legs above the hocks and on the body.*

7 BREEDING COCKER SPANIELS

Breeding a litter of puppies from your Cocker Spaniel can be very rewarding, but it can also be costly and time consuming. Each pregnancy will also put your bitch at risk, so you need to consider the pros and cons very carefully. You should not breed from your bitch if she has any health issues or faults that she would perpetuate in her puppies. With Cockers, the most important illnesses to avoid are early deafness, slipping patellas, eye conditions, and hernias. You will want to make every effort to ensure that the puppies that you breed have sound temperaments, are healthy and are good examples of the breed. You will also want to make absolutely sure that your puppies go to good homes.

Before you go ahead and breed your litter, you would be well advised to ask yourself some serious questions. Do you have the time to look after your litter until they go to their new homes (around eight weeks)? Are you knowledgeable enough to advise your puppies' new owners about the various aspects of caring for their puppies, including their diet, training and health problems? Can you afford the veterinary bills for your bitch's ante-natal care and for her litter? Do you

know enough to help the bitch during her labour? Could you afford for your bitch to have a caesarean section if she needs one? Are you equipped to raise the puppies with everything they need including worming, vaccinations and socialisation? Most importantly of all perhaps, will you be able to place your pups into good homes and would you have the resources to take puppies back if the homes you sold them to prove unsuitable?

Many people breed from their Cocker Spaniel bitch because they would like to keep a puppy for themselves and most bitches sail through whelping and very much enjoy having puppies. You should not breed from your Cocker until at least the third time she comes in season, at approximately eighteen months old and ideally before she is three years old. Her final litter should be born before she is eight years old.

THE STUD DOG

The demands on dog breeders grow increasingly complex to ensure that future generations of dogs are bred responsibly. The over-riding consideration is the health of any potential puppies. This is particularly

73

important when you are looking for a stud dog. He must have a good temperament, good health and be a good example of the Cocker Spaniel. If your bitch came from a reputable breeder, go back to them and ask their advice about what stud dog to use. It is always best to use a proven, experienced stud dog. Predicting breed type and characteristics requires experience. If you are new to dog breeding then you should seriously consider joining an appropriate breed club where you will be able to meet and talk to some very experienced breeders.

You should certainly take the time to go and see the dog that may become the father of your puppies. You should also be prepared to show your bitch's pedigree to the owner of the stud dog so that they can approve of her. Ask what the stud fee is and what conditions will be included; for example, do you get at least two matings if necessary and if your bitch fails to have puppies, does the stud fee cover a free return? Most stud dog owners offer this. You then need to work out when your bitch will be in season and when the puppies will be born.

There is a lot of time and work with puppies, so make sure you are going to be available to give it when they are born.

MATING

New breeders need to concentrate on finding out when their bitch comes into season. If you don't realise until your bitch has been in season for several days, it may be too late. This is disappointing if all the plans have been made. You will need to check your bitch virtually every day for the start of her season. The first sign is the vulva swelling. Some bitches' vulvas swell and do not show any signs of red discharge, others will show very little red discharge. Count from the day her vulva becomes swollen, just in case she is a bitch that has clear seasons.

Once your bitch is showing colour wait until the discharge becomes paler until you take her to be mated. You can check this by using either a white tissue to dab the vulva morning and night to determine the colour change, or you can put a white cover on her bedding so that you can monitor the colour change. If your bitch does not show any colour change you will need to count the days after she comes into season; ten to twelve days after coming in season is probably the best guide. However, some bitches are ready to mate after just six days into their season and have produced puppies from this mating, but this does not happen very often.

Once the bitch has been mated, you must keep her away from other male dogs until she is completely out of season. It would probably be wise to keep her away from any male dog all the time she is in season.

First-time breeders can also be

nervous. Not everyone is aware that mating dogs "tie" or "lock" together during mating, on average usually for about twenty to thirty minutes. Sometimes dogs are locked together for hours, although this is very rare. It is usual to have your bitch mated twice, approximately forty-eight hours apart; once this is done take your bitch home and keep her secure and quiet.

Occasionally a bitch will, after being mated, have a red discharge from her vulva, even as late as three to four weeks after mating. This usually indicates that the bitch is in whelp and there is activity within the womb. In the early days of pregnancy nothing should be changed, so treat her normally.

PREGNANCY

A bitch is usually pregnant for sixty-three days or nine weeks, but you should be prepared for her to give birth up to five days early or four days late. You may be able to see that your bitch is pregnant from about five weeks, although some bitches do not show until seven weeks. Early signs of pregnancy are a thickening around the waist. Her vulva may remain slightly swollen and there may be a slight colourless discharge. She may also lose her appetite, and she may be sick. She may also become very quiet. On the other hand, she may show no signs at all but still could be pregnant. If you can see signs of her pregnancy very early, this may indicate that she is

having a large litter.

As soon as you know that your bitch is pregnant you need to change her diet from approximately five weeks

ABOVE: *Once your bitch has been mated, keep her away from other male dogs.*

onwards. As the puppies grow bigger she will not be able to eat as much as she needs in just one feed. It is advisable to split her food into at least two meals a day, and up to four feeds a day towards the end of her pregnancy. It is very important to keep your bitch well nourished so that she will have the energy she needs to give birth. In the final two weeks, your bitch's exercise should be supervised so she is not overtired. Gentle exercise is good for her but car journeys should probably be avoided. You should also stop your bitch jumping down from anything higher than two feet tall. Towards the end of the pregnancy your bitch will probably have a sticky clear discharge from her vulva; this is normal. Any other colour is not and may mean she could be aborting her puppies and needs to be seen by your vet as soon as possible.

WHELPING

As your bitch's due date approaches you should decide where she will give birth. This needs to be somewhere comfortable, quiet and warm (around 21 degrees centigrade or 70 degrees Fahrenheit). It would be sensible to inform your veterinary practice that your bitch is due to whelp. Then if you do need to consult them in the middle of the night they are better able to give you any help you need.

When your bitch goes into labour the best thing to do is to sit quietly near her and give her comfort and reassurance as and when she needs it. Her body temperature will change from her normal body temperature of 37.2 to 38.6 degrees centigrade (99 to 101.5 degrees Fahrenheit). This stage of labour can last as long as twenty-four hours, and she may pant and tremble and dig up her bedding and look totally distressed. Don't worry, this is quite normal. You should only offer her clean water at this stage, as many bitches vomit during labour. You may also wish to trim the long hair around her tummy and hindquarters to stop this getting in the way. Your bitch will then go into the next stage when strong contractions will start. She will start to push as they increase in intensity. Her first pushes will be light and get much stronger. Your bitch may also pass a water bag which will then break, producing a clear greenish liquid. Soon after this the contractions will get stronger and a puppy should be born within twenty to thirty minutes. This second stage of labour can last between three and twenty-four hours with puppies being born within twenty minutes of each other, but there can be up to two hours between puppies. Mum will usually clean the puppy of its covering membrane and bite through the umbilical cord. Some puppies are born tail and hind feet first, but this isn't a problem. Each puppy should be followed by its afterbirth or placenta.

the bitch is straining, or a placenta is retained, you should call your vet immediately. He can give your bitch an injection that will result in the bitch expelling any retained afterbirth.

When your bitch's labour is finished, you should get the mother something to eat and drink, and help her to go outside and relieve herself. A drink of goats milk with honey or glucose dissolved in it will ensure that she has enough fluid on board to produce milk for the puppies.

You should remove and replace the soiled nest covers and then give the new family some time alone. Your bitch will probably want to sleep while she suckles the puppies. This first milk is very important as it contains colostrum that contains the mother's antibodies and will protect the pups until they are old enough to be vaccinated. It may be wise for your vet to see the bitch and puppies soon after whelping. He can check the puppies for any abnormalities.

If your bitch is busy delivering the next puppy, you should remove the membrane from the puppy (so that he can breathe) and dry him with a clean facecloth. Rubbing will encourage him to take his first breath and crying helps to clear his airways. You should also tie a piece of heavy thread around the cord approximately one inch from the pup's body, then tie another knot a little further from the first and use clean scissors to cut the cord between the knots. Be very careful not to cut too close to the puppy, and dip the end of the cord in tincture of iodine or chlorhexidine.

The third stage of labour is the passing of the placentas. You should count them to make sure that none are retained in the uterus. Some bitches eat the placentas which contain nutrients that help her body to recover. If you are unsure how things are going,

AFTER THE WHELPING

If your bitch isn't interested in taking care of her puppies and doesn't show any concern for them for more than an hour you may need to take over looking after them. You should also consult your vet for advice. Hand-rearing may be necessary, especially if the bitch doesn't seem able to produce any milk. Other bitches are fantastic mothers and don't even want

ABOVE: *The mother will need to eat well to produce enough milk for her growing puppies.*

to leave their puppies so that they can go to the toilet.

It is very important that your new mother eats well. After eating the rich afterbirths your bitch may refuse food for a while and may go off her food altogether. You need to tempt her with some tasty treats. It is often preferable to feed your bitch several small meals a day, consisting of really good quality food. She will also need to eat well to produce enough milk for her growing puppies.

ECLAMPSIA

Eclampsia is a life-threatening condition that results from the bitch's loss of calcium during pregnancy (making the puppy's bones) and in her milk. It usually happens within a few weeks of her giving birth. Smaller dogs with large litters have an especially high risk of the condition. It can be avoided by a good diet in pregnancy. Symptoms of this frightening illness (which can start very quickly) include panting, drooling, vomiting, restlessness, muscle spasms, convulsions, breathing difficulties, heart problems and seizures. Eclampsia is a serious medical emergency and your dog will need urgent treatment, which will usually include calcium. This can be given intravenously. Once treated, your bitch should make a full and speedy recovery. However, the puppies should be fed for at least twenty-four to thirty-six hours. If there is any recurrence, she should not suckle the puppies again.

The New Litter

The new puppies will start to grow a day or so after they are born. They should put on a few ounces in weight each week. Their eyes should open within twelve or fifteen days. The first teeth appear at around twenty-eight days. Their pink noses will soon start to go black!

WEANING THE PUPPIES

You should start weaning the puppies between the age of two and three weeks. Worming is also one of the most important things at this time. Puppies can be born infected by worms and worms will prevent them from thriving. The puppies will need worming at two weeks of age. This can be done with a liquid puppy wormer that your vet will supply. They should be wormed twice more before the age of eight weeks. As you start to wean your puppies, you can give them saucers of warmed puppy milk several times a day. When the puppies have accepted the puppy milk you can move on to solids. This could be canned puppy meat or dried food formulated for puppies. This should be fed warm. Dried food should be soaked until the puppies' teeth are stronger when it can be fed dry. Your puppies should also have constant access to fresh water. This is particularly important if you are feeding dried food as this can make the puppies very thirsty. By the age of eight weeks your puppies should be fully weaned and eating and drinking independently. They will then be ready for re-homing.

Summary

With his happy temperament and waggy tail, the Merry Cocker has become an increasingly popular pet over recent years. Gentle and loving, Cocker Spaniels are happy to both work and play with their human families. Although Working Cockers tend to have higher levels of energy than Show strains (who often have calmer temperaments) both types need plenty of exercise and mental stimulation to fulfill their potential.

Photo by Lynn Gould p 9;
Photo by James Gower p 37;
Photos by Sue Casebourne pp 1, 3, 5, 14,17, 18, 28, 36, 38, 39, 40, 41, 43, 47, 48, 51, 58, 61, 62, 68, 75, 80.